A BOSTON'S WORLD

D1279100

A Boston's World

by
Anchor's and RJ's Special Beau

writing as

MICKEY

To Winnie
who treats me like a dog
but I still love her anyhow.

Printed in the United States of America
by
Concept II Graphics & Printing, Incorporated
9004H Yellow Brick Road
Baltimore, Maryland 21237
800-788-3196

ISBN 1-879295-27-X

photography credits
Elizabeth Saunders, p. 20
Edmund Wadhams, p. 31
Marion Chambers, p. 40
Linda Nyborg, p. 42
Ariel Skelley for the E. S. of Va. S.P.C.A., p. 47
Marilyn Randall, p. 57

Book Design by Kevin S. Lowery

My Life,
An Autobiographical Sketch
by Mickey

I'm told I was born in the middle of winter in Fayetteville, Pennsylvania. All I recall about the first weeks of life is being cared for tenderly and lovingly by Joanne Hale. At eight weeks, I moved to Marilyn and Norm Randall's warm, comfortable home in Accokeek, Maryland. It was there that I got a taste of the show circuit as *Anchor's and RJ's Special Beau*. Looking back, I remember that I enjoyed traveling around that summer and exchanging sniffs with lots of interesting dogs, but the show ring routine got old in a hurry. At the end of the summer, I was somewhat relieved when the Randalls said they would find me a non-show home because they thought my lower jaw might not be developing exactly right.

One day that fall, two strangers named Anne and Floyd Nock appeared at our door in Accokeek. They'd heard from Elisabeth McNeil, another Boston owner in Crownsville, Maryland, that I was for sale, and they drove all the way from the Eastern Shore of Virginia to see me. They had a good smell, and I liked them right away. They talked to me softly and rubbed me gently under the chin where I like to be petted. For what seemed like a long time, they stood around talking about me.

When I heard Marilyn Randall explaining to them what I liked to eat and how I liked it fixed—in the blender mixed with warm water, NOT MILK, that's for babies—I knew they were serious about taking me home. Then, because they'd never had a show-type dog before, Norm showed them the fine points of grooming, and Marilyn kissed me goodbye. As my new owners and I walked out to their van, I could see there was a brand new dog crate in the back. But do you know what? All three of us got in the front seat, and I snuggled down in Anne's lap for the ride home. I already missed my Boston buddies, but it felt good for the first time in my life to be top dog.

The Randalls admit that they would never have sold me if they'd known I could write. Too bad I never got my paws on their computer, but I couldn't get to it because it was located in a little alcove off from the kitchen where I lived. Such is life.

From the top of a filing cabinet in our loft, I can see far and wide.

In my new home with the Nocks, I have access to a computer almost any time. It's up in the loft area that's one of my favorite places. Here I can work at the computer, sleep in an easy chair, or jump to the top of a file cabinet in front of a high-off-the-floor window. I love having a birds-eye view of the outdoors. Right outside the window, birds flutter about and squirrels scurry around in the treetops. If I look down, I can see on land, pickups, cars, people and dogs (even cats) inching along on the street; on the water, boats returning from crabbing and fishing and joy riding with their wakes curving off behind them. I love to look out from my loft window and see the whole world in motion.

In case you are wondering if I took the pictures in the book, the answer is *NO!* Delayed timers don't work very well for me, and besides, I have trouble closing one eye to look through a viewfinder. I'm lucky the Nocks agreed to do the photography. That left me free to concentrate on the writing.

Why do I write limericks? You'll never guess. It's like playing ball. With limericks, I play with an idea the way I play with a ball. To find the best ideas and words for a limerick, I look at the possibilities dancing around in the air, snatch the best ones out of the blue, toss them around, jump at them sideways, take pretend bites, and finally grab whatever I want, running with it as fast as I can. For me, it's much more fun than regular poetry. And it beats prose all to pieces.

But back to my story. Let me tell you about the next big event in my life. Winnie, my friend and companion, came to live at our house late the next spring. (Winnie's real name is *Nock's Parsonpride Winnie*; her dad is *Ch Eu-Bet I'm the Parson's Pride*; her mom, *Stella Polaris Whitney*.) Again, Elisabeth McNeil located her all the way out in Hudson, Ohio, at the Reverend Bruce Trethaway's house. I really envy Winnie—she had a real airplane ride in a kennel attendant's carry-on before she was three months old. She rode all the way from Ohio to B.W.I. Airport where Jodi Ghaster, the McNeils' handler, met her plane and took care of her until the next day when we drove up to Crownsville to meet her. But now, lest I let too many cats out of the bag, I'll stop this introduction except for one more comment.

Because Eastern Shore dogs and people always want to know as much as possible about your ancestry, I think I should say a little more about my canine family. My canine mother is *T-Party's Sugar Magnola of RJ*, and my dad is *Ch Debohara's RJ Duff Stuff (Dusty)*. Here's a picture of Dusty, my dog dad, at the Baltimore show with Mrs. Hale. Floyd is holding me so I can see what's going on. Friends think I bear a strong resemblance to Dusty. He and I agree.

Jodi Ghaster introduced little Winnie to me. (top)

At the Baltimore show, I had a nice visit with Dusty. (bottom)

9

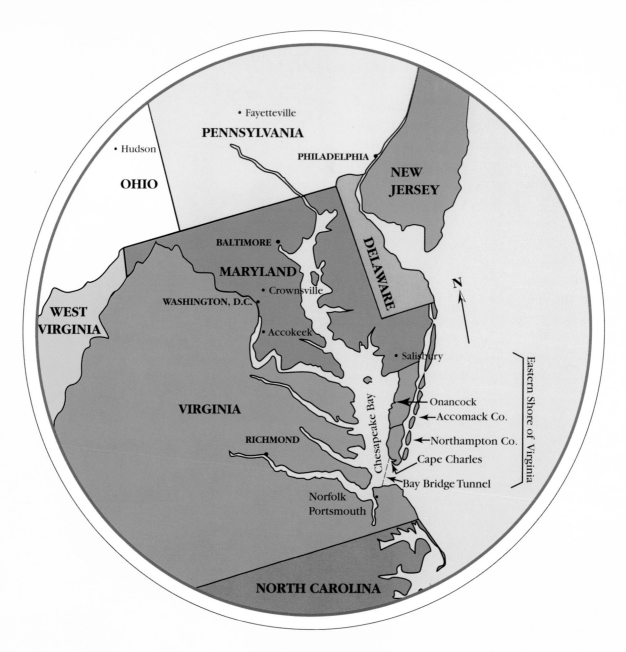

My World

I. Winnie

After being without a playmate for almost a year, I was some kind of happy when Winnie came to live with us. Loveable, coy, unpredictable, energetic—that's Winnie! She's more fun than 25 balls! To say she nearly drives me to distraction with her teasing is stretching it a little, but it's almost true. I must confess that sometimes, I tease her, too.

She was a just a baby, 10 weeks old, when I first laid eyes on her. As soon as Jodi introduced us, we felt we'd been close friends forever. On the ride to Onancock from Crownsville that day, we were both so keyed up we couldn't stop talking. Winnie told me about her family in Ohio, and I told her about my early days in Pennsylvania and Maryland.

> As soon as we drove up our drive,
> She seemed to detect we'd arrived.
> I showed her her crate—
> (By then it was late)—
> She lapped up some water, then dived. . .
>
> Head first, in a flash, into bed
> And slept like a dog nearly dead.
> I watched over her—
> (This small traveler)—
> And looked to the days then ahead.
>
> You see, I was pleased as could be
> Just having a sister with me.
> It's what I had wished—
> Each time at my dish—
> I'd eaten a meal lonesomely.

I'll never forget that first week. Mom and Dad and I all tried to help Winnie feel at home. We introduced her to our neighbors, and took her across the Bay (that's what we call driving over the Chesapeake Bay Bridge Tunnel to Norfolk and Portsmouth) to meet our grandmother, uncle, aunt and cousins. And we took her to see our vet. She wasn't sick or hurt, but we knew if she could feel Dr. Cameron's gentle touch and hear her soothing voice, she wouldn't dread going later on when she might be sick or need a shot.

Winnie works on a marrow bone.

Mostly I've taught Winnie, but she's also taught me a thing or two. Take bone anchors. She'd never even heard of a marrow bone, much less seen or tasted one before she came to our house. But right away, she figured out a lot of ways to keep a marrow bone from scooting around when she's gnawing it. She anchors it on somebody's shoe or against a piece of furniture. And if that doesn't work, she puts her foot through it's hole and clamps down on it.

Winnie keeps me guessing all the time. Maybe that's what's so appealing about her. One minute, I think I understand her. The next, I'm befuddled by her actions or barks. I am fortunate to have known her in her puppyhood. I've heard that's when most attitudes for life are formed. Seeing her grow up has given me a better understanding of what makes her tick than if she'd come to live with us when she was grown.

We aren't kin to each other, I mean, not close kin. I guess way back, all Bostons are kin, but for us, not for the past hundred generations or so. However, we think of ourselves as brother and sister. That's as it should be since we're living under the same roof and have the same owners. People who look at us and say, *"Oh, what cute twins,"* ought to have their eyes examined. We don't really look anything alike!

Sometimes, my nose gets a little out of joint when people we meet on the street make a lot over Winnie and don't pay much attention to me. I don't hold it against them—she really is as cute as any puppy could be. When that happens, I just remind myself that Winnie's my pride and joy—and I don't feel jealous any more.

Where is Winnie?

She's fast as an energized flea,
She zips like a charged bumblebee
To hide underneath—
A chair, or beneath—
A ruffle or bed canopy.

"You're not any rival for me!
You can't even run down a flea!"
I wouldn't dare bite—
She's such a dear mite—
"Look out! Here I come, bumblebee!"

And then, I will suddenly see
A little black nose, that's the key,
An ear or a paw—
Or part of a jaw—
She's trying my patience with glee.

Winnie takes great pleasure in hiding from me.

Winnie's Hairdo

I'm happy with hair that is straight,
But Winnie's not sure of our fate.
She's asking this tyke—
Just what it is like
Just how does it feel with the weight. . .

Of hair that is lengthy and curled
That covers your body in swirls,
She's more or less sure—
A Shih Tzu's coiffure—
Is much more becoming a girl. . .

Than hair that is straight, very straight,
She thinks that a perm might inflate
Her own self-esteem—
I try not to scream—
But try to be calm and sedate.

I say to her, *Cool it, my dear,*
Accept who you are, the whole schmear,
Be thankful you're you—
I like your hair-do—
Who wants to be clothed in cashmere. . .

In winter and summer as well?
The wintertime part would be swell,
But, oh, when it's hot—
You'd roast on the spot—
In summertime, it would be hell!

Winnie wonders if she would like a Shih Tzu hairdo.

14

Squishing a Ball

For Bostons, a ball is pure bliss.
You'll see that it's true for this Miss.
Though she is quite young—
She's having great fun—
Just squishing her ball in a squish.

Squishing a ball is Winnie's specialty.

15

Bath Time

Miss Winnie, each chance that she gets,
Will run to the tub to get wet.
She'd bathe ev'ry day—
If she had her way
While I only scrub with regret. . .

Say, once, maybe twice in a year!
It's soap plus the water I fear.
And when I'm not dirty—
When I'm looking purty—
There's simply no reason to gear. . .

My thinking to washing my coat.
So if I detect a bath note,
I run off to hide—
Somewhere on the side—
That's hidden from two-legged folk.

And thus I'm exempt from the pain,
The nonsense, the folly, the strain
Of taking a bath—
Plus its aftermath—
Which seem to me wholly insane!

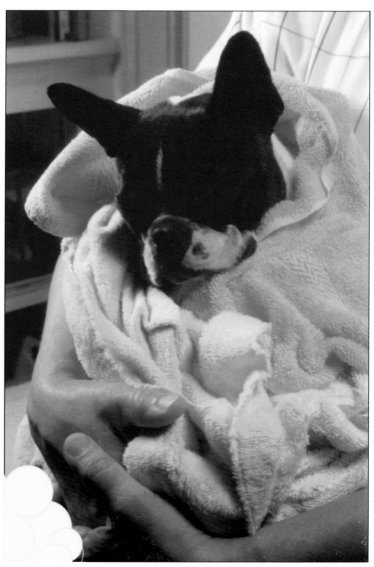

Winnie enjoys bath time.

Forty Winks

I've heard of some folks who can sleep
Without even counting their sheep
While sitting upright—
Or standing full height—
It must be a difficult feat.

But Winnie's a definite pro
At vertical sleep. What a show!
In rhythm, she snores—
(Our Dad, she adores)—
"Two bugs in a rug"—apropos.

I don't see how she does it, but Winnie can sleep in any position.

Head Start

We took little Winnie to school
To study some puppyfied rules.
(It's really *Head Start* —
Pre-school's counterpart.)
I knew that my Winn was no fool. . .

But I didn't know she would be
The top-of-the class nominee.
    She mastered the stuff-
      With nary a huff—
        And got an authentic degree.

      We think it will put her in line
       To by-pass first grade in due time.
      Because she's advanced—
     In heeling and stance—
First graders, she'd quickly outshine.

Winnie is second from left in her kindergarten class.

Nurse Winnie

When somebody's under the weather,
It's Winnie who acts like a tether
To whoever's sick—
The hurt, she will lick—
She works like a nurse altogether.

She watches the patient with care
From down on the floor, in a chair
That's close, very close—
From whence she's engrossed—
Concerned for the patient's welfare.

An eye on the patient, she keeps,
And if he should let out a peep,
She yelps a loud yelp—
Or runs to get help—
She watches him wake or asleep.

I'm proud she is such a good nurse.
To nursing, I am not averse
But I just don't know—
I'd get a zero—
Enabling hurts to disperse.

While Winnie is nursing bedside,
I'm doing my watching outside.
It's what I can do—
So, that I pursue—
With genuine Bostonese pride!

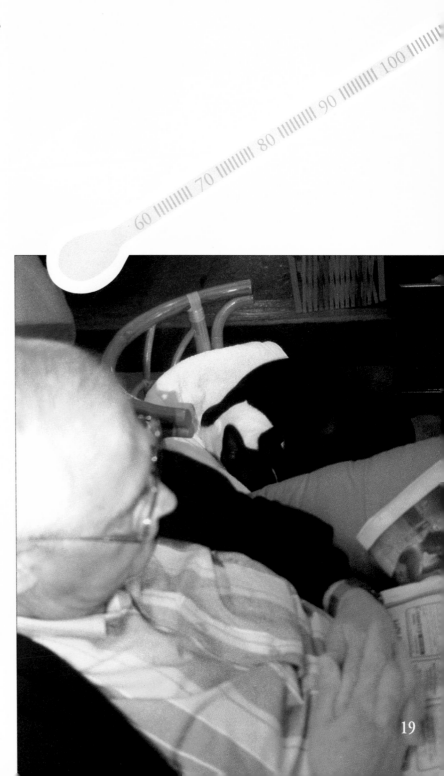

Nurse Winnie keeps an eye on her patient.

19

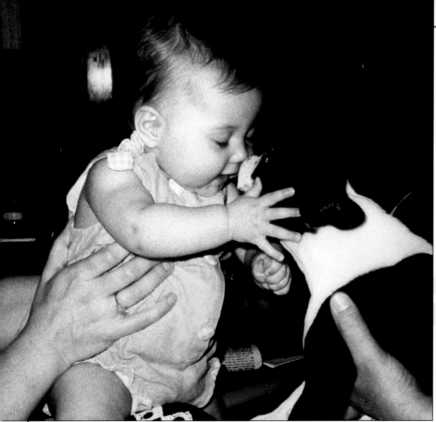

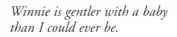
Winnie is gentler with a baby than I could ever be.

Planting a Kiss

With children, we'll play, any day
In whatever way that they say.
But I would say *maybe*—
Concerning a baby—
I'd not want a tearful display. . .

That possibly might come about
If one of them tickled my snout.
I'd try not to move—
So I could help prove—
A Boston's an out-and-out scout!

But truth of the matter is this,
Afraid I would frighten this miss,
I'd agitate some—
And be frolicsome—
Instead of just planting a kiss.

Miss Winnie is gentler by far
With babies, she's right on a par,
She moves not a hair—
So tots, she won't scare—
With little ones, Winnie's a star!

II. Teamwork

Before Winnie arrived, I lived the typical life of an only child. I was pampered and loved, played with and disciplined. Life for me was good, but I longed for a canine playmate. You can share certain things with people but not everything.

Now that Winnie and I are usually together, I sometimes wonder what I did with my time before she came. To be truthful, I'm lost when I'm not with her. I'll admit she bosses me around too much, but that's okay. I let that get started when she was a baby. To keep peace, I've just let her keep on making a lot of the decisions. Now and then, when she gets completely out of line or when something really matters to me, I just take charge.

If it's not too hot in the summertime, we like fast-paced games like chasing balls, playing with pull toys and racing like wild Indians. But slow games are fun, too, summer and winter, especially if there is a little teasing involved. We're especially good at naps and take lots of them.

The sofa pillows really appeal to us.

21

A Twin-engined Jet

A'slogging through mountains of snow
Is something I'd rather forego,
But just for a while—
(No more than a mile)
I'll chase any toy that you throw.

Young Winnie pretends she is grown;
She leaps for whatever is thrown.
But she cannot match—
The way that I catch—
She rarely can bag one alone.

At times, she will manage to get
A hold on the toy—then we're set
With true Boston grip—
To race and to rip—
Like somebody's twin-engined jet.

But mostly she runs alongside
And tries not to fall down or slide.
I think she does well—
This Bostony belle—
To nearly keep up with my stride.

*We don't get much snow,
but when it comes,
look out!*

22

As Best We Can Fit

Whenever the sun shineth bright,
We look for a sunbeam of light
That streams through a door—
(Warm sun, we adore)
'Cause Winnie and I take delight. . .

In feeling the warmth that it brings.
In winter, fall, summer or spring
We follow the sun—
Where it has begun—
And where, later on, it will swing.

We bask in its path, what a treat!
To Bostons, a sunbeam is sweet.
We lie or we sit—
As best we can fit—
To feel ev'ry bit of the heat!

If we are chilly,
heat from the sun warms us up.

23

Boston Alarm Guard

With Winnie and me standing guard
Surveying the house and the yard,
We shouldn't have spent—
A single red cent—
On anything bought to retard. . .

The entrance of somebody who
Would knock down our things all askew
And carry off booty.
'Cause we are on duty—
We'd give any thief what he's due!

We've already worked out a plan,
At first, I would waylay the man,
Then Winnie would bark—
(Her bark has a spark
To make any thief freeze and stand). . .

While I, on the side, would attack
And tear up his legs with a thwack,
I'd bite him so hard—
He'd let go his guard—
He'd run and he'd never come back. . .

To here, where we live, on the Shore,
He'd nevermore walk past our door
Remembering how—
Two Boston bow-wows—
Near pinned him down flat on the floor.

He's lucky he fled in the night.
You see, Boston Terriers fight
Whenever we sense—
A thug's evidence—
We're fiery as hot dynamite!

We don't need an alarm system.

24

Boston Billy Goat Gruff

Our playing is oftentimes rough.
I like to be Billy Goat Gruff,
And Winnie's a troll—
(A suitable role)—
So both of us have to be tough.

The stage can be anywhere set,
But using a chair's the best bet.
Though Winnie's a mite—
She has a mean bite—
Which makes her a genuine threat.

Not simply pretending to play,
But having to keep her at bay
From up on the bridge—
(My chair anchorage)—
Adds infinite fun to our day!

Sometimes we play rough.

House-warming Present

*As a gift to a friend, we offer
to be their watchdogs for an afternoon.*

Miss Winnie and I, we've agreed,
Are giving a present (no fee),
A service of sorts—
(No playful cavorts)—
We'll function as guard dogs for free!

We'll listen for question'ble sounds,
And, if there's a crook lurking 'round,
We'll scare him to death—
With snorified breaths—
With growling and barking profound,

We'll sniff out his lousy old trail,
And pin him for sure, without fail,
We'll hold him at bay—
And with him, we'll stay—
'Til cops come and take him to jail!

We're usually sugary sweet,
But that's not the story complete,
We're vicious as well—
If trouble, we smell—
A Boston T. dog can't be beat!

We're better, by far, than a hound!
In sniffing around on the ground
It's true, very true—
The nose-length issue—
Is not a real issue all 'round. . .

Employing our noses, though short,
Accepting the noses we sport
We use what we've got—
Though that's not a lot—
At work and at various sports!

Ushering

We're thinking of looking around
To see if a job can be found.
Yes, Winnie and I—
Are agile and spry—
Our Bostony trademarks abound.

Some excellent practice, we've had,
It's not just an ev'ryday fad
That's with us today—
Tomorrow passé—
And we are quite good, I might add. . .

At pulling a towel or sheet
For us, it's a genuine treat.
The corners we catch—
With a Bostony latch—
And then we can run a blue streak.

For ushering jobs, we'll apply,
I'm certain we'll well classify.
We'll pull out with pride—
The sheet for the bride—
We think not a bride will deny. . .

The service we plan with a smile,
Of working the wedding-route aisle.
No tux must we rent—
For formal events—
We're already dressed in high style.

Sometimes we pretend we are ushers pulling the aisle sheet for the bride.

You Called?

You called? We're engaged, you might guess.
We're busy, away from our desk
A break we must take—
From being awake—
Please leave us alone. I don't jest!

There're times when we're in a tailspin.
A little white lie is no sin.
Don't you think it's fair
We rest in the chair?
And later we'll say that we're in!

28

*Sometimes we're too busy to
answer the phone or the door.*

Pull-toys

We're really quite agile at pulling,
I try to be fair, not be bullying.
We both prefer hose—
Or any soft clothes—
Not anything scratchy or wooly. . .

Just looking at wool makes us itch,
It throws in our playtime, a hitch
And tastes really gross—
Like a medicine dose—
And causes our noses to twitch.

Stockings are a marvelous pull-toy.

29

III. Our Family and Friends

I'm yawning because I'm tired of posing for the family picture.

In addition to Winnie and me, our family is made up of Anne and Floyd, and Sarah and Levin, their adult children who live far away in Georgia and Washington. Although we don't see Sarah and Levin often, we love them whenever they come for visits. And you can be sure we love Anne and Floyd dearly because they are so good to us. Sometimes I wonder what it would be like to live somewhere else, but whenever I do real day dreaming, I'm right here at home!

Many wonderful people and dogs have come into my life and Winnie's because of my family. I always enjoy meeting new people and getting to know them. I've heard you can tell a lot about a person by the look in his eyes or the tone of his voice. The voice thing is probably true. Maybe the eyes part. But what a person looks like or what he wears doesn't make much difference to me one way or the other. The best way for me to know what somebody is like is to see how he plays. If he gets down on your level, right on the floor, he's okay. Next best is when he lets you jump up in his lap. Sometimes a person won't benddown at all but stands up tall like a giraffe. In that case, I just check him off.

Winnie and I have people favorites as well as dog favorites. By and large, most people are polite. Some even speak to us, and a few seem to understand what it's like to be a little dog. As for dogs, it's mostly personality that counts. And to some extent, it's size, too. When we see an 80-pounder, we automatically shake in our boots. You can't blame us. An 80-pounder might be as gentle as a lamb, but if he's not, we're in big trouble. You'll understand why most of our close canine buddies are in the 5-to-25 pound catdogegory. In the next few pages, we'll introduce our family and some of our special friends, both canine and human.

Her Den is a Dog's Camelot

Our grandmother loves us a lot.
A marvelous basket, she's got
That's brimming with toys—
For dogs to enjoy—
Her den is a dog's Camelot!

We play with her toys by the hour
And use up our energy power
To race all around—
Her cozy compound—
And try not to knock down her flowers.

We lay out a fast thoroughfare
That runs over two of her chairs
Her sofa as well—
All set parallel—
It's sort of an oval affair.

The ends are the challenge for us,
We bridge them though yes, perilous,
With gigantic leaps-
(Momentum we keep)
That land us on track with no fuss.

She also lets Winnie and me
Play hide-and-then-seek, oh what glee!
We race at top speed—
Not hitting, indeed—
Our grandmama who's 93.

Our grandmother lets us do anything we want at her house.

32

Uncle Barry doesn't mind getting down on our level.

Pitching Words

Our uncle's a newspaper man,
The writer for all of our clan.
He's tall as can be—
But notice the key—
To why we're his resolute fans:

Aware that we're not very tall,
He kneels down as if he might crawl.
And that may be why—
Though he's a tall guy—
He writes about things, large and small.

When we horse around in his yard,
We play we are his bodyguard.
We also pretend—
We're newspaper men—
Reporting from countries afar. . .

Like China or Turkey, exotic.
We like to write things idiotic
While playing with words—
That may be absurd—
But, rolled into shape, sound hypnotic.

Our uncle plays ball using blurbs,
A game that, with us, is preferred
The absolute most.
He keeps us engrossed—
As long as he keeps pitching words.

Aunt Evie loves big dogs and little ones.

A Baby Boston is So Sweet

Her fam-i-ly has a dog now,
Or rather, there're two, one's a cow,
Not really, I joke—
I don't mean to poke—
Ridiculous-ness, but I vow. . .

A Rottweiler looks like to me
A mighty big dog nominee,
Though Max is no cow—
His toes touch my brow—
And that is the truth. Winn agrees.

Our auntie, some decades ago,
Had two little dogs in a row.
Yes, Tammy and Lil—
For years, filled her bill—
And captured her heart tremolo.

We think, when she's looking at us,
A vision of their impetus
Unfolds in her mind—
And we sort of bind—
The tie of their life's exodus.

We're hoping some day she will find
Another small dog, any kind,
But possibly one—
As companion—
Who fits in the Boston design.

A Representative of People, Dogs, and Cats

Our cousin has cats of her own
And that is a fact we bemoan,
But Winnie and I—
Hereby testify—
Whenever she comes to our home. . .

She's gentle and loving and kind
To dogs of a Boston incline.
She talks with us both—
Takes note of our growth—
Enjoys the games we design.

We're happy her int'rests include
The whole world-of-dogs latitude,
Because it is true—
The work she pursues—
Has bearing on Accomack's* mood.

She works for the counties and state
Including the rules that dictate
The citizens' rights—
Their problems and plights—
Pertaining to county mandates.

So back to my premise of sorts,
Though Ellen has cats, she's a sport
Who represents well—
The folks where they dwell—
Plus felines and Bostons that snort!

*Our county, the northernmost of the Eastern
Shore of Virginia's two counties

Winnie couldn't stay out of Cousin Ellen's lap.

35

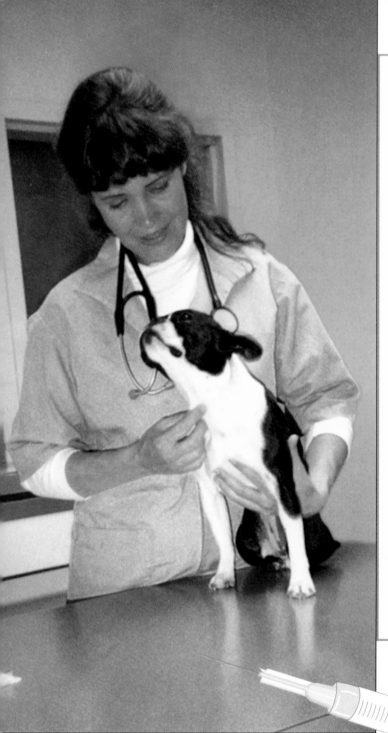

Our vet always tries to make our hurts feel better.

Dr. Paula, Our Vet

Our vet makes us well when we're sickly.
She usually works on us quickly
With pills or a shot—
That she will allot—
Her shots are not bad, they're just prickly.

We, both of us, love all the fuss
She lavishes gently on us.
When we're feeling bad—
Or just a bit sad—
She always takes time to discuss. . .

The ins and the outs of a hurt,
Explaining, meanwhile, in concert
The treatment we'll get—
So we aren't upset.
Our thinking she knows to divert. . .

With stories and laughter and jokes
That entertain us and our folks
While she ladles out—
The most direct route—
To fixing what's hurting or broke.

Our Babysitter

Our sitter is Catherine C.
The best in the world, we agree.
A ray of sunshine—
We think she's divine—
She's top-of-the-line company.

She treats us like royalty dogs
And takes us on heavenly jogs.
To be in her care—
Is beyond compare—
We're happy she's our petagogue.

Our babysitter is especially understanding.

37

Our neighbors love us as if we were their own.

Next-door Neighbors

A walk on a leash, we adore.
We see lots of people—and more,
The dogs and the cats—
And their habitats—
It's buckets of fun to explore.

Our neighbors, at times, let us go
Whenever their walk's apropos.
We love when they call—
'Cause we have a ball—
From home to the town gazebo. . .

And on for an hour or two
To sections of town that are new.
Not only the walks—
But, too, we have talks
With Norma and Doug, quite a few.

Most days they will stop in to speak,
To tell us the news, bright or bleak,
The cats they have spotted—
The notes they have jotted—
To tell us when next we will meet.

And also they come in to play
Most any old time of the day.
Though we're prejudiced—
I promise you this—
They're wonderful friends—come what may!

Winnie's Namesake

A name is important as heck.
That's clearly the reason we trek
To Northampton County—
A trip paramounty—
For Winnie, her name, to connect. . .

With one other Winnie of note,
Who lives in Cape Charles. She devotes
Her time to the arts.
I think, in her heart
My Winnie would like to promote. . .

The cause of all dogdom in art!
She says it would warm up her heart
If hung on the walls—
Were dogs large AND small
Not only the Labradors, smart,

But also some Dachshunds and Pekes,
Some Cockers and black Schipperkes.
Some small Beagle hounds—
In splotched black and browns,
And also some breeds that are chic.

So if, in the future, you find
Somewhere in this gallery design
A picture of pups—-
With Boston make-ups—
It just might be Winnie's and mine!

Winnie talks with Winnie Bell, her namesake.

Nickie's Four-poster Bed

A playmate, we have, who's named *Nick*,
And Winifred's dad is called *Mick*,
But no other Joe—
Do I really know—
Whose name rhymes with mine. Fiddlestick!

This fellow is *Nicholas* boy.
He's really a bundle of joy,
A mouthful of fluff—
A brownish-buff puff—
Who looks like a mechanized toy!

Our nighttimes are spent in our crates.
It's true that we think they are great,
But Winnie and I—
Would never deny—
The chance to be like candidates. . .

For sleeping aloft on a bed
With pillows to cushion our heads,
On blankets and quilts—
Like *THE Vanderbilts*—
Relaxing on comforts outspread!

When we, to our dreamlands, descend,
This Nickie, our little-est friend
Ascends ev'ry night—
To four-poster height—
His bed, we can scarce comprehend.

Nickie sleeps in a real bed.

My Teacher

I thought it was some kind of cool
Attending a dog-training school.
We socialized some—
I made some new chums—
And also I memorized rules.

My teacher was really superb.
No fooling, an addle-brained bird
Could learn how to fly—
Up high in the sky—
Just tuning her in, word for word.

I want you to well understand
That she and her partner are grand!
And I'd give a paw—
If I knew the law—
Like Lady who works on command. . .

As easy as gnawing a bone.
I'll have to confess that I groaned
When I was engrossed
In watching up close
Some birds that had fluttered and flown

When she was explaining a rule,
And I wasn't thinking of school,
But most of the time—
My thinking was primed—
At not being counted a fool.

It's true that she took lots of care
To help ev'ry one of us there
To be, down the line—
Without fret or whine—
Obedient, NOT a nightmare!

Lady and Linda Pruitt are a great teaching team.

41

A Definitive Nose

My classmates, at school, by and large
Were nearly the size of a barge
Except for Miss Mollie—
A miniature collie—
A *Sheltie's* her breed, and she's charged. . .

With plenty of vigor and vim,
She's classy, attentive and prim,
We like to keep step—
With plenty of pep—
We're, both of us, healthy and trim!

She has a definitive nose
Which helps her, I'm sure when she goes
To root out a bone—
That she has once owned—
And also when she is supposed. . .

To clean up some dining room crumbs.
Or do other stuff that's humdrum,
She's sharp as a tack—
I've watched and kept track—
I think she's a real sugar plum!

Mollie is one of my school classmates.

Our Adoption Counselor

She thought of two Bostons, not one,
And carefully focused her gun
On Mom's and Dad's minds—
Until they would find—
First me, then my Winn, for a chum.

The details she quietly chased
Promoting her "two-Boston" case
'Til Mother and Dad—
Agreed they would add—
Not one dog, but two, to their place.

So Maddy's the reason we're here.
If she hadn't been engineer,
Who knows where we'd be—
In what company—
To think of it causes us fear.

She visits us often, or calls,
And keeps us supplied with nice balls.
Wherever she goes—
She looks high and low—
For balls that are smushy and small.

If balls are too smooth, they will slip,
And we cannot get a good grip.
A ball's acid test?
Some roughness is best—
Cause then we can grip with our lips. . .

As well as with teeth chomping down
While running around and around.
It's hard to explain—
The fun balls contain—
Believe me, a ball is profound!

To Maddy, we constantly bark
Our thank-you's, deep down in our hearts.
We love our landscape—
We're fixed up shipshape—
We're, both of us, happy as larks!

Maddy comes to play ball with us almost every day.

43

We're Her Precious Angels

When people say, *"Puppies, let's play,"*
If they are up five feet away
From us on the floor—
It's really a chore—
To jump up and stretch a long way.

But most of our friends realize
That people and dogs socialize
More easily when—
The people can bend.
That shouldn't be any surprise.

Myree had a Boston for years,
But now, we're the dogs in her sphere.
Because we are handy—
She thinks of her Brandy—
When playing with us little dears.

Whenever she visits, she brings
Some presents to us, some play-things.
She calls us her angels—
Her precious-est angels.
To play with Myree makes us sing!

Myree calls us her little angels.

What strong teeth you have!

Playing Rough

A dentist would probably flip
If ever he witnessed the grip
That Verrill displays—
When he and Winn play—
You'd think that his teeth would all rip...

And rattle and fall on the floor
To be in his mouth nevermore.
But he has a smile—
That glows for a mile—
With <u>all</u> of his teeth, underscored. . .

Aligned in an enviable form,
They're even and straight, uniform.
No chips and no cracks—
They're all there intact—
They don't even look a bit worn.

Most dentists we know preach a lot
With stuff like, *The teeth that you've got
Are valuable tools—
So follow the rules—
Look after them, friend, or they'll rot!*

This fellow named John is our friend,
This guy is a comedien,
He likes to play rough
He'll huff and he'll puff
He's hoping his teeth will not bend. . .

Whatever the dentist might say.
I know if Miss Winn had her way
They'd stay in on forever—
'Cause she would stop never—
'Til doomsday, she'd play and she'd play!

Winnie nestles down in Phil's lap.

Playing in Our Dreams

A writer of fiction is Phil,
He has a remarkable skill,
The stories he writes—
Are pure dynamite—
His work is NOT run-of-the-mill.

And Cindy's remarkable, too,
She's helping our hospital crew
To reach for perfection—
In ev'ry direction—
By thinking of ideas new.

They're two of our loving-est friends
They're able to well comprehend
The way that we feel—
With passion and zeal.
With Cindy and Phil, we would spend. . .

A lot of our time if we could,
They're not, though, in our neighborhood.
Whenever they come—
We talk with them some—
Because we are both understood,

Then play 'til we run out of steam
And feast on some strawberry cream,
Alas, in their laps—
We rest and take naps—
While playing some more in our dreams.

Santa Claus

The S.P.C.A. made a deal
That had for us, lots of appeal.
It bargained with Santa—
Some wishes, he'd grant~a~—
We'd get to see Santa for real!

He'd come in a week, we had heard
So both of us quickly conferred,
We'd try to be good—
We knew that we should—
If truth could be told with our words.

Remember the text of the song?
We tried and we tried, all week long,
♪ *Not naughty, but nice*— ♪
We took the advice—
And did all the rights and no wrongs!

The day of our meeting arrived,
We hopped in the car for the drive
And waited in line—
Where we were assigned—
And managed, somehow, to survive.

As soon as we sat in his lap
We knew that this jolly old chap
Was one of a kind—
With traits that combine—
To put him, for us, on the map.

We chatted a minute or two,
Then bid him a speedy adieu,
The others still waiting—
Were all agitating—
We said to him, *merci beaucoup!*

We felt just as free as two hounds
Out sniffing around on the ground.
We now could relax—
Be wild maniacs—
And get into mischief profound!

For a whole week before we saw Santa, we tried to be good.

47

IV. Winnie's Blank Verse

You'll notice that the next several pages are not written in limericks but in blank verse. That's Winnie's doing. I should have known she wouldn't enjoy writing limericks because she won't play ball even halfway right. I think it's *won't*, not *can't*. She *could* fetch a ball decently if she wanted to, but she'd rather bug me when I'm running with it. All she does is snatch the ball out of my mouth after I've made the catch.

Sisters can be exasperating at times. I love Winnie dearly, but sometimes I can't understand her. Being of a younger generation, she's into newer styles and newer methods. Take haircuts. She wants a feather trim where the white of our collars meets the brindle/black of our coats. I'm happy with a punk cut. With collars. She loves a hot pink collar. I stick to black. Take baths. She's got to have a fancy blow-dry job even though she's been well toweled after a bath. I just run around to dry off. True, too, in writing. She's for blank verse. I write limericks while she's cranking out unrhymed stuff. Truth of the matter is, sometimes I think she just wants to be different.

When I started working on this book, Winnie begged me to let her co-author it. She was just learning the alphabet, and I was sure she wouldn't know enough to write anything by the time it went to press. She pestered me, saying things like *You need a woman's point of view. Lots of people don't like rhyme, Mickey. Give them a break.* Finally, to get her off my back, I gave in. *Okay, Winn you can do two, maybe three pages max. But if you nag any more, not even that!* I never dreamed she'd stray so far afield from my way of writing.

I always try to be patient with her. I realize she's not much more than a baby even though she thinks she's as grown up as I am. I guess, considering her tender age, she does well. Yes, she has promise. I'm sure of that. Maybe there's something to this blank verse. Perhaps I'll try it sometime.

Winnie springs over a big snowdrift.

Brothers

Brothers?
Nice to have around.
My brother looks after me
Not too much, mind you.

Whenever I have a hurt
And must go to the vet,
He's at my side
Licking my hurt
Telling me it will be all better.

We love to
Tease, taunt,
Joke, play,
Roll, tumble,
Pretend the same pretendings.

When I call him *Mickle*
He's furious
Barking back
Winifred—that I detest.
But then we growl it up
and wrestle some more.

When day is done,
When play time is over,
He's always there
Telling me
Come, little one,
Rest your head on my shoulder.

Mickey is my best friend.

50

Mickey says he is king of the table at the end of our sofa.

Mickey's Heat Lamp

We Bostons are cold natured.*
It's a fact of life.
No big deal.
But when I'm chilly,
I'd almost fight for

A purring radiator
Soft warm mittens
Toasty sun rays
Fluffy towels from the dryer
Puppy chow mixed with hot stew
A heat lamp
Even a plain old lamp.

And fight I must for Mickey's table
Where he likes to lie
Under a lamp.
He thinks he is
Goat-on-the-mountain
On the table text to the sofa.

Lucky am I to get a paw on his table
Much less two paws
Plus a few more inches.

*By cold-natured I mean our body temperatures that tend to be low: cold-natured doesn't refer to our ~~person~~doggy-alities which are warm.

51

The big wing chair is great for snoozing.

Parallel Naps

Snoozing in a easy chair is
A favorite pastime for Mickey and me,
Curled up close together,
Snoring contentedly in harmony,
The warm cradle of his back, my pillow.

Fanciful dreams
Float through my head
Bouncing balls
Tasty treats
Tumbling puppies
Loving pats
Not all for me,
For me AND for Mick.

Should snarling cats
Angry dogs
Stinging wasps
Or cold whipping winds
Cloud my dreams,
I need but think a whimper
And Mickey chases them away.

I feel safe, completely safe
With Mickey at my side.
I know he'd take on a bear
Of a dog to protect me.

V. My Personal Life

When I started this project, I thought I'd write mostly about Winnie. Watching her grow up has been a real experience. It wasn't long before I realized that in order to get a full picture of her, I'd have to include some stuff about the two of us such as our common interests and activities because there is so much we do together. But still I held the line. There would be nothing personal about me. Who cares about a grown Boston Terrier? Nobody. It's different with cute little Winnie. I can't imagine any dog or person not interested in her winsome, sometimes cunning ways.

As I was working along with her as my main focus, I kept hearing that people gobble up autobiographical info about people-authors whose books they are reading. That got me to thinking. Maybe the same would be true for readers of a canine-author's work. Boston owners might especially enjoy reading about me. So one day, when I was in a floating-on-a-cloud-of-marrow-bones mood, I tried my paw at writing down some of my feelings—my hopes, dreams, observations. It was fun. I mean not really fun fun but satisfying fun. Winnie urged me to keep at it. She's always encouraging me to try new things. She could tell it was making me feel more confident.

This last chapter gets down to nuts and bolts.

In a jack-size ball, that's how this chapter came about. Take it or leave it!

I managed to stay awake the whole time our cousins were here.

Sunday Afternoon

This looks like a portrait that's posed,
My father is dressed in church clothes,
And I'm at attention—
Not even to mention—
My black-and-white coat, how it glows.

But really, it's Sunday at four.
Our cousins had come to the Shore
To visit with us—
They sat and discussed—
Affairs of the world and lots more.

They talked about relatives, too
Plus people that all of them knew,
It went on and on—
A real marathon—
And Winn fell asleep in a shoe!

But I, all the afternoon long,
I didn't do anything wrong,
I managed to stay—
Awake the whole day—
I slept not a wink 'til they'd gone. . .

And then, in a minute, I dashed
Right straight to my crate where I crashed.
It really felt nice—
In my paradise—
I fell fast asleep in a flash!

Kissing

I'm careful as careful can be
When kissing's suggested to me,
I make the decision—
Without supervision—
Depending on who's vis-a-vis.

A favorite person is Renia,
Of Pekingese pus, she's the queena.
Of Bostons, as well—
We Bostons can tell—
In order, we're next on the scene.

She teaches first graders at school,
Her outfits are fashionably cool,
Her shirt is in color—
Plain words would be duller—
A kid or a dog or a mule. . .

Could learn without trying to learn
Without giving learning a turn,
'Cause pictures plus words—
So I've overheard—
Make learning a happy concern.

With dogs, she is quite democratic.
Her pups have TV automatic,
Plus A.C. and heat—
Their digs can't be beat—
It's country club style—plutocratic!

So now, you should understand why
With Renia, my friend, I'm not shy.
We're like kissing cousins—
My kisses, a dozen—
I'm always prepared to supply!

Renia and I whisper sweet nothings to each other.

Playmates

I'd rather not tell you it's true
But yes, I'm the doll baby who
Is willing to play—
With Lisbeth today—
Her usual playmate has flu.

It suited me fine to pretend
That we are the closest of friends.
She's gentle and kind—
Today, she is mine—
I'm hoping the day will not end.

*It's better than
you might think
to be Elizabeth's
doll baby.*

My First Valentine

Isn't Shelly beautiful?

All lonesome, was I, and afraid
The very first move that I made
But one special pup—
Enlivened me up—
And helped all my cowardice fade.

She played with me, pulling a sock
While barking some words Jabberwock.
We romped on the floor—
And barked at the door—
Whenever somebody would knock.

I miss her whenever I play,
Though Winnie is fun in her way,
If Shelly were here—
We'd race in high gear—
And have a fantastical day.

Perhaps down the road, Shelly dear,
(When there is a show that is near)
You'll work out a way—
To come here and play—
I'll look up, and you will appear!

But meanwhile, my mem'ries will do,
I live a full life the year through,
But, yes, I'd delight—
If you were in sight—
If you should come out of the blue,

I'd romp and I'd run all around,
I'd probably act like a clown.
We'd feast upon stew—
Plus biscuits to chew—
And I'd take you out on the town!

A Sprung Kangaroo

The toys that we have are diverse
Some balls, large and small, an old purse,
Some bones that we chew—
(We have quite a few—
A stockpile, in fact, that we nurse.)

We'll play with a stick or a mop,
A frisbee, a stocking, a sock,
And if there's no toy—
We find special joy—
Inventing a game that's *ad hoc.*

Sometimes, when a toy will not do,
(It happens right out of the blue)
I just want to run—
To be venturesome—
To run with the wind and pursue. . .

I love to leap like a deer in the snow.

A feline (pretend) or a squirrel.
I play that I'm free in the world
To go anywhere—
On life's thoroughfare—
Cavorting and jumping in swirls.

I race like a Greyhound I knew,
Or a cheetah escaping the zoo,
I leap like a deer—
Without any fear—
And spring like a sprung kangaroo!

My Footstool

The needlepoint footstool is mine
It raises me so I can find
The action outside—
The herons that glide—
The butterflies, birds and canines,

The rabbits that lurk in the grass,
The squirrels that leap around fast,
The slinking tomcats—
The muddy muskrats—
I stand by the hour, alas,

Enjoying the sights near the Bay.
I can't figure out, buy the way,
Why Winnie, my friend—
Will simply not spend—
Some time looking out every day.

*Up on my footstool, I can see out much
better than from down on the floor.*

59

Bird Watching

I look at the birds by the hour
A-flitting from bower to bower.
They fly where they please—
With absolute ease—
Enjoying their natural power.

I wonder just how they can fly.
I try to jump higher than high,
But I don't take flight—
Don't soar like a kite—
Like little birds up in the sky.

Though flying is something I'd like,
I'd scare every grownup and tyke.
A Boston on wing—
Would cause quite a ring—
With humans and canines alike!

I wonder what it would be like to fly like a bird.

My Daffodil

My daffodil came from Tasmania.

Most flowers, I take or I leave,
Concerning their names, I'm naive,
But one is a star—
It came from afar—
It's story is hard to believe.

It hails from Tasmania's land.
My auntie, a daffodil fan,
She found it for me,
My own fleur-de-lis,
A miniature daffodil grand.

And would you believe that its name
Is *Mickey*, the same that I claim?
So you can see why—
Excited am I—
It grows in our garden terrain.

It's liking our climate and rain,
It's bloomed in our seasoned domain,
As soon as its plume—
Was ready to bloom—
I told the whole world of its fame.

61

A Boston's Domain

Chasing a ball is a Boston's domain.

I'll run 'til I'm blue in the face
Forever enjoying the chase
Of catching a ball—
(With balls, I'm enthralled)
I'll match any terrier's pace,

And possibly come out ahead
Because of the times I have led
With Winn at my side—
In motion, full stride—
Attempting to win by a head.

A ball can be any old size,
A real one or one improvised,
The game is the same—
A Boston's domain—
Is running and catching the prize!

Stand-Off

Old Jethro, I watched by the hour.
If I had a chance, I'd devour
This whole blessed cat—
We're have quite a spat—
Meanwhile I'm content just to glower.

This feline is handsome enough
Though surely no soft powder puff.
Just look at that ear—
It's evidence clear—
That Jethro's a fighter who's tough.

So, when I am itching to fight,
I look at that ear on his right
And simmer right down—
Just give him a frown—
And otherwise act quite polite!

Jethro and I respect each other's prowess.

School Is Like a Club

Obedience training's a snap.
I don't understand all the flap
Concerning the rules—
In a dog training school—
It's simply a neighborhood rap. . .

When some of us dogs gather round,
A Golden, A Schnauzer, a hound,
A Dal and a mutt—
Who has a crewcut—
'Most all of the breeds can be found.

It's sort of a club in a way
'Cause all of us hanker to play,
When class, though, begins—
We go in tailspins—
To practice the rules of the day.

At times it is hard to obey
Whatever command is conveyed.
Though I really try—
To quickly comply—
There're times when I just want to play.

My mind starts a'dreaming of fun,
Like springing away in a run,
Or jumping around—
Or being a clown—
Or guarding an old garrison.

But usually, you can be sure
My motives are noteworthy, pure,
I'm doing my best—
With all of the rest—
My *citizen* rank to secure!

You can spot me and my teacher in the middle of the front line.

Tribbie, My Flame

A frizzly rope fills the need
In pumping up Bostonized speed.
A tug-of-war game—
With Tribbie, my flame—
Means fun without fail, guaranteed.

If Tribbie is slow to join in,
I bounce in a measured side-spin,
Then, her, I entice—
With barks, once or twice—
As she moves along with a grin.

We dart here and there as we play.
I bark out to her, *Bombs Away!*
Then break in a run—
Like shot from a gun—
And gather a posy nosegay. . .

That's really a bit of a stick,
Or maybe a bug she can lick,
A leathery leaf—
A torn handkerchief—
Or some other tasty tidbit.

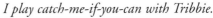

I play catch-me-if-you-can with Tribbie.

Porches

A porch, I must mention, is fun!
I play it is my garrison,
Protected around—
By fortified ground—
And I'm the commander—with gun!

To watch from a porch, all the world,
The people and children and squirrels
Who pass back and forth—
To south and to north—
The robins that fly in a whirl. . .

Is something I really enjoy,
It's better, almost than a toy,
'Cause I am engrossed—
Complete, uttermost—
In watching the hoi polloi,

The activities of the town,
(Close up on the street and outbound)
The boats in the creek—
The bikes on the street—
Surrounding the harbor compound.

I sometimes imagine at watch
(While Winnie is playing hopscotch—
She's simply too young—
To look out far flung—
She's just got to grow up a notch). . .

That I'm in command of the town,
I listen for any new sound
And sniff at the air—
So I can compare—
The usual smells all around. . .

With anything new on the scene
That's off in the daily routine,
And also I look—
(I read in a book—
That people who look really mean. . .

Are often more likely to wrong)
Yes, often, I check out a throng
And pick one or two—
Who're rough, through and through,
Who look like they do not belong.

To sum it all up in a word,
A porch is a pastime *preferred*
By dogdom at large—
'Cause we are all charged—
To stand up and bark and be heard!

66

Our neighbor's porch is a first rate patrol post.

Treats

Whenever I hear the word *treat*,
I look for a goody to eat.
My tongue activates—
My mouth salivates—
It matters not if it is meat,

Or if it's a morsel of cake
A cookie or crunchy cornflake
But I must admit—
The finest tidbit—
That causes my tummy to quake,

The absolute, ultimate treat
Is something that's heavenly sweet,
A specialty cheese—
And Winnie agrees—
That creamy cream cheese can't be beat!

Cream cheese is my favorite treat.

67

Life and Death

We, both of us, love to have fun
Just messing around with our chums,
One place that we go—
Has three in a row—
Three Pekingese mops on the run.

It seems only yesterday, five,
Yes, five of these pups were alive
Enjoying life—
With minimum strife.
Today, there are three who survive.

It saddens me greatly to think
That suddenly, quick as a wink,
Our comrades and friends—
Can come to the end—
And never again eat or drink!

Though clearly they're no longer here,
I'll always remember the cheer
They heaped upon us—
'Ere their exodus—
Though vanished, I feel they're still near.

I'm sure there's a heaven for pets
Because I still think a *quintet*
Is playing around—
The Davis compound—
Those Pekes, I shall never forget!

Hanging out with Pekes is like dodging powered mops.

68

Work and Play

We're both of us partial to preachers
As well as to resolute teachers,
Our grandfather Bryant—
Was highly reliant—
The Methodist Church was his feature.

My Winnie's a Luth'ran by birth,
She lived out her first weeks on earth
In a minister's home—
She gnawed her first bone—
In Trethaway's Ohio berth.

A good Presbyterian friend
Who knows how to say an *amen*
Is Anthony Dick
At pulltoys, he's quick—
He keeps us in tune with the trends. . .

That surface and come to the fore
Concerning the clerical corps.
Just watching him play—
Reminds me the way—
We've heard that our grandpa of yore. . .

Was called *Joe E. Brown** many years
Because he could quickly shift gears
From matters quite stern—
To joking concerns—
And still be completely sincere.

It seems not to matter at all
What church one attends overall,
But what seems to count—
What's most paramount—
Is whether a guy can play ball. . .

Tony Dick plays rope with Winnie.

And have a good time down the road
As well as to shoulder his load
Whoever he is—
Videlicet, viz°—
A dog or a preacher hallowed!

* Joe E. Brown was a radio/movie comedian in the
  1930s and 1940s.
° *Viz* is the contraction for *videlicet* meaning
  it's easy to see.

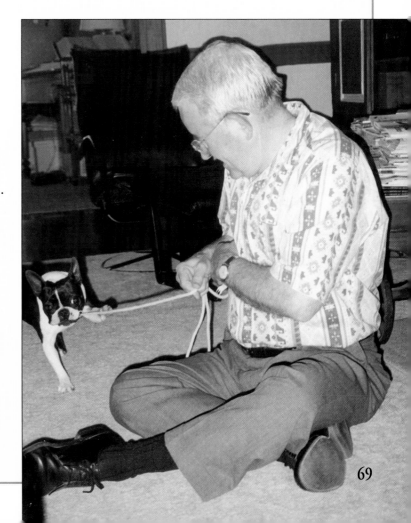

Computers

Computers are wonderful tools,
We've mastered enough of the rules
To write pretty fast—
(By paws, in contrast—
Forever, it takes, until you'll. . .

Dismiss even trying to write,
'Cause forming the letters just right
Is tiresome at best—
So we keep abreast—
With WordPerfect writing on site.)

We patiently wait for our turns
To enter our thoughts and concerns.
When two-legged folk—
Take breaks for a Coke—
Our canine-world rights, we affirm!

Just one little leap, and we're there
From sidelines to swiveling chair,
On line with the muse—
Expressing our views
To people and dogs ev'rywhere.

*Winnie waits her turn
for computer time.*

ADDENDUM
Mickey, the Writer
by Anne Nock

Soon after Mickey came to live with us, he started writing—not just for the sake of writing—but as a means to an end. It happened like this. Although he had adjusted well to our home, he seemed lonesome now and then. Assuming he missed his former playmates, in particular his buddy, Shelly, we asked a friend to bring her miniature wirehaired Dachshund, Tribbie, to play with Mickey from time to time. Soon Mickey and Tribbie were fast friends, but an occasional pensive expression clouding Mickey's face indicated to us that he still longed for Shelly. (Later, Mickey would tell us he thought about going back to Maryland to visit Shelly, but he didn't mention it at the time.) It was shortly before Valentine's Day, just three months after Mickey came to live with us, that we discovered valentine limericks he was writing to his two sweethearts, Shelly and Tribbie.

After this propitious beginning, Mickey began to write birthday, get-well, sympathy, and graduation cards to people friends as well as dog friends. A happy fellow by nature, Mickey has a remarkably vivid imagination. Meanwhile, Winnie, having become a member of our family, was helping Mickey gain a measure of self-confidence that he had not known before. In what seemed like no time at all, Mickey's writing branched out from short greeting card thoughts to essays of several pages, the first two being *It's a Dog's World* and *A Dog's Philosophy of Life*.

Although Mickey has no graduate degrees, he feels that his diverse background and well-rounded, basic education give him a stronger grip on the meaning of life than the average dog-on-the- street or the typical dog in the show ring. His credentials include fundamental training in socialization skills with Joanne Hale; show ring etiquette under the tutelage of Norm Randall; graduation with honors from SPCA-sponsored "Canine Good Citizen School" under instructor Linda Pruitt; and certification as a fully-licensed member of "Therapy Dogs International." Winnie is also a licensed "Therapy Dog" and a "Canine Good Citizen" graduate (though not with honors). Both Winnie and Mickey have attempted to join the "Dog Writers Association of America," but because membership is not open to dogs for some inexplicable reason, they must be content with DWAA association through my membership.

Mickey is well aware he will never enjoy the glamour or fame of two other Canine-American writers of the twentieth century, but this doesn't bother him at all. He acknowledges that the late Fala Roosevelt (1940s) and the late Millie Bush (1990s), both presidential reps of the highest order, are due their fame because of the high office over which they presided. Everyone knows that Fala is memorialized for all time at the FDR monument in Washington and has been further honored with the recent re-publication of his noted literary work, *The True Story of Fala*. And Mickey's contemporary, the distinguished Millie Bush, is fondly remembered by the American public for her winning autobiography, *Millie's Book*, and for the strategic role she played at the big White House during George Bush's presidency. Even young Buddy Clinton has thrown his hat in the writing ring. Too bad he has had to share the honors with a cat.

Mickey speaks in an all-American way from an everyday perspective. It is his hope that dog-lovers and dogs everywhere, especially Bostons and Boston lovers, will gain pleasure from his literary efforts.

INDEX

A portion of the proceeds from *A Boston's World*
will benefit

Boston Terrier Club of America Rescue

The Boston Terrier Club of America's Project Rescue pairs homeless Bostons with loving families. For information, call 724-883-4732, contact via e-mail at btcaresc@greenepa.net, or write Box 52, Mather, PA 15346

and

The Eastern Shore of Virginia SPCA

The Eastern Shore SPCA provides shelter, food and care for homeless animals, as well as sponsors a Spay/Neuter Assistance Program and educational programs for dogs and their owners. For information, call 757-787-7385

"This book is a metaphor for humans. It is a much deeper read than appears on the surface — a wonderful light-hearted escape that speaks of having fun just for the heck of it, of accepting the idiosyncrasies of others, of making the best of what you have, and of dreaming dreams each day of your life. It also touches on the more serious side of life — the universal need for friends, the reality of death, the importance of faith, and the value of appreciating the meaningful things in life. There's much more in Mickey's mind than meets the eye. He has penned a lesson in life for people as well as for dogs."

Peggy Swan, Licensed Professional Counselor

Concept II Graphics and Printing
A MARYLAND CORPORATION

A host of friends, both dogs and people, helped me with this book. I am appreciative to all of them—those who are the subjects of photos and limericks, those who let me use their pictures, and those who offered ideas for improving my book. Especially I am indebted to my friend/editor, Phil May, who stood in for Dad when he was ill and helped me ready A BOSTON'S WORLD for publication after Dad died.

Petey with Fala at the FDR Memorial

A BOSTON'S WORLD might never have happened without the encouragement and assistance of Petey (Stallings), my new Scottie friend. Lucky for me that Petey's dad, Jimmy Stallings, gave her a free leash in matters pertaining to my book. (Petey is the Scottie who has created Fala Roosevelt's *My Story, the Official Fala Coloring Book*, for today's kids.)

When Petey teamed up with Winnie and me (like the Three Musketerriers), she helped us sniff out some wonderful trails that we could never have found without her. One of those was Concept II Graphics and Printing, Inc. up in Baltimore on a street named, if you can believe it, "Yellow Brick Road." Once we got there, we didn't find Toto, but we did find wizards whose magic brought my book to life. Licks, kisses, and nuzzlings to Kay and Al Johnson, Kevin Lowery and all the staff at Concept II!

Mickey